Date: 2/21/18

J 796.334 HOU
Stewart, Mark,
Houston Dynamo /

HOUSTON DYNAMO

BY
MARK STEWART

NORWOOD HOUSE PRESS

Chicago, Illinois

NORWOODHOUSE PRESS

P.O. Box 316598 • Chicago, Illinois 60631
For more information about Norwood House Press please visit our website at
www.norwoodhousepress.com or call 866-565-2900.

Photography and Collectibles:
The trading cards and other memorabilia assembled in the background for this book's cover and interior pages
are all part of the author's collection and are reproduced for educational and artistic purposes.

All photos courtesy of Associated Press except the following individual photos and artifacts (page numbers):
The Upper Deck Company LLC (6, 10 bottom, 11 middle), Topps, Inc. (10 top, 11 top & bottom, 16),
The Mundial Group, Inc. (22).

Cover image: Robert Chambliss/Associated Press

Designer: Ron Jaffe
Series Editor: Mike Kennedy
Content Consultants: Michael Jacobsen and Jonathan Wentworth-Ping
Project Management: Black Book Partners, LLC
Editorial Production: Lisa Walsh

LIBRARY OF CONGRESS CATALOGING-IN-PUBLICATION DATA
Names: Stewart, Mark, 1960 July 7- author.
Title: Houston Dynamo / By Mark Stewart.
Description: Chicago Illinois : Norwood House Press, 2017. | Series: First
  Touch Soccer | Includes bibliographical references and index. | Audience:
  Age 5-8. | Audience: K to Grade 3.
Identifiers: LCCN 2016058201 (print) | LCCN 2017005792 (ebook) | ISBN
  9781599538631 (library edition : alk. paper) | ISBN 9781684040827 (eBook)
Subjects: LCSH: Houston Dynamo (Soccer team)--History--Juvenile literature.
Classification: LCC GV943.6.H68 S74 2017 (print) | LCC GV943.6.H68 (ebook) |
  DDC 796.334/64097641411--dc23
LC record available at https://lccn.loc.gov/2016058201

This publication is intended for educational purposes and is not affiliated with any team, league,
or association including: Houston Dynamo, Major League Soccer, CONCACAF, or the
Federation Internationale de Football Association (FIFA).

302N--072017
Manufactured in the United States of America in North Mankato, Minnesota.

CONTENTS

Words in **bold type** are defined on page 24.

In soccer, star players often go by a one-word nickname. In this book, we use the nickname followed by the player's (*full name*).

Mauro Manotas congratulates Andrew Wenger after a goal in a 2016 game, while Sheanon Williams listens to the fans cheer.

MEET THE DYNAMO

A "dynamo" is a person who never gets tired and never gives in. What a great name that is for a soccer team! Just ask the Houston Dynamo. The Dynamo are members of Major League Soccer (MLS). They have some of the sport's smartest and most loyal fans. They adore soccer. Many play it, too. They show their love to the Dynamo players at every game.

The Dynamo joined MLS in 2006. Many of its players had been members of the San Jose Earthquakes the year before. Their skill and teamwork helped the club win the **MLS Cup** in 2006 and again in 2007. The club's great players include Brian Ching, Pat Onstad, and **Eddie Robinson**.

Brian Ching scans the field for an open teammate during a 2012 match against D.C. United.

The Dynamo's stadium brings fans very close to the action.

Best Seat in the House

The Dynamo play their home games in a stadium built in 2012. It is a beautiful building that holds more than 22,000 fans. Many seats have a view of the Houston skyline. The club took to its new field right away. They did not lose a match there until 2013. Their 35-game **unbeaten streak** set an MLS record.

COLLECTOR'S CORNER

These collectibles show some of the best Dynamo players ever.

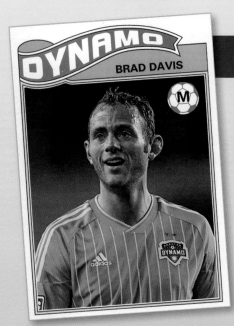

BRAD DAVIS

Forward/Midfielder
2006–2015
No player in MLS history had a better left foot than Davis. His passes and free kicks were always on the mark.

PAT ONSTAD

Goalkeeper
2006–2010
Onstad's diving save during the MLS Cup **shootout** gave Houston the 2006 championship.

BRIAN CHING

Forward

2006–2013

Ching scored four goals in the Dynamo's first game. His 56 goals are the most ever by a Houston player.

DWAYNE DE ROSARIO

Forward/Midfielder

2006–2008

De Rosario was a big reason Houston won championships in 2006 and 2007. He had led the Earthquakes to MLS Cups in 2001 and 2003.

WILL BRUIN

Striker

First Year with Club: 2011

Bruin was a college star before joining the Dynamo. He quickly became one of the top scorers in MLS.

WORTHY OPPONENTS

The two best soccer teams in Texas are the Houston Dynamo and FC Dallas. The cities are about four hours apart. Fans travel to away games to cheer for their team. The Houston–Dallas matches are called the Texas Derby. The winner each season takes home an old-time cannon. Dynamo players look forward to these games all year.

Try as he might, Carlos Gruezo of FC Dallas cannot steal the ball from Houston's Collen Warner.

13

CLUB WAYS

Soccer players are known for their superstitions. When clubs in Europe start a winning streak, sometimes the players stop shaving for good luck. Sports teams in the United States do this, too. They grow "playoff beards." The Dynamo players grew lucky beards when they won the MLS Cup in 2006 and 2007. They grew them again in 2011 and made it all the way to the finals!

Brad Davis leaps to celebrate a goal during the 2006 playoffs. He and teammate Wade Barrett were both working on their lucky beards.

ON THE MAP

The Dynamo bring together players from many countries. These are some of the best:

1. **Brad Davis** • Saint Charles, Missouri, USA

2. **Dwayne De Rosario**
   Scarborough, Ontario, Canada

3. **Boniek Garcia** • Tegucigalpa, Honduras

4. **Alejandro Moreno** • Barquisimeto, Venezuela

5. **Giles Barnes** • London, England

6. **Joseph Ngwenya** • Plumtree, Zimbabwe

7. **Leonardo (*Jose Leonardo Ribeiro da Silva*)**
   São Paulo, Brazil

NORTH

WEST — EAST

SOUTH

MAP OF NORTH AND CENTRAL AMERICA

The Dynamo's home stadium is in Houston, Texas.

1

2

3

4

5

6

7

WORLD MAP

Ricardo Clark wears Houston's home kit during a 2016 match. The club's crest is on his shirt and his shorts.

KIT AND CREST

The Dynamo players wear orange uniforms for their home games. The shirts and shorts have touches of black, white, and blue. Their away kit is black with bold orange stripes. The team crest is a shield with the name of the team. It also shows a soccer ball and a star. The star is a symbol of Texas.

WE WON!

The Dynamo faced the New England Revolution in the MLS Cup in 2006 and again in 2007. In their first meeting, Brian Ching headed in the tying goal in overtime. He then scored the winning goal in an exciting shootout. In 2007, New England led the match, 1–0. Joseph Ngwenya and Dwayne De Rosario scored late in the second half for a 2–1 win.

Wade Barrett shows the 2006 championship trophy to the fans. The Dynamo won the MLS Cup in 2006 and again in 2007.

The Dynamo won five tournaments and league championships in their first 10 seasons!

MLS Cup

2006

2007

Carolina Challenge Cup

2006

2007

2015

Dwayne
De Rosario

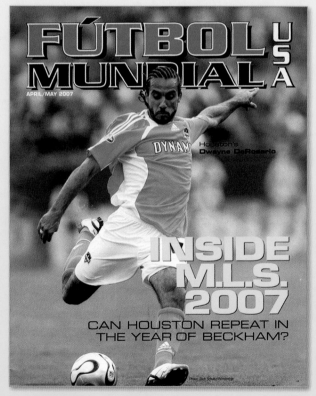

These stars have won major MLS awards while playing for the Dynamo:

2006   Brian Ching • Goal of the Year

2006   Brian Ching • MLS Cup Man of the Match

2006   Ricardo Clark • Best XI Midfielder

2006   Dwayne De Rosario • Best XI Midfielder

2007   Dwayne De Rosario • MLS Cup Man of the Match

2007   Dwayne De Rosario • Best XI Midfielder

2007   Eddie Robinson • Best XI Defender

2009   Geoff Cameron • Best XI Defender

2009   Stuart Holden • Best XI Midfielder

2009   Pat Onstad • Save of the Year

2011   Brad Davis • Best XI Midfielder

MLS Cup
The championship game of Major League Soccer.

Shootout
A tie-breaker used mostly in championship soccer matches. Each club gets five penalty kicks, with the team scoring the most awarded the victory.

Unbeaten Streak
A series of matches a club either wins or ties without a loss in between them.

Photos are on **BOLD** numbered pages.

About the Author

Mark Stewart has been writing about world soccer since the 1990s, including *Soccer: A History of the World's Most Popular Game.* In 2005, he co-authored Major League Soccer's 10-year anniversary book.

About the Houston Dynamo

Learn more at these websites:
www.houstondynamo.com
www.MLSsoccer.com
www.teamspiritextras.com